The Adventures of Wild Willy

TRUE STORIES FROM 1940 - 1980

WILMA R. FORESTER

Copyright © 2025 Wilma R. Forester.

All rights reserved. No part of this book may be reproduced, stored, or transmitted by any means—whether auditory, graphic, mechanical, or electronic—without written permission of both publisher and author, except in the case of brief excerpts used in critical articles and reviews. Unauthorized reproduction of any part of this work is illegal and is punishable by law.

Library of Congress Control Number: 2024903895

ISBN: 979-8-89419-665-7 (sc)
ISBN: 979-8-89419-666-4 (hc)
ISBN: 979-8-89419-667-1 (e)

Because of the dynamic nature of the Internet, any web addresses or links contained in this book may have changed since publication and may no longer be valid. The views expressed in this work are solely those of the author and do not necessarily reflect the views of the publisher, and the publisher hereby disclaims any responsibility for them.

One Galleria Blvd., Suite 1900, Metairie, LA 70001
(504) 702-6708

Contents

Introduction 3
1. The Missing Nickel 7
2. The Treasured Dungeon 13
3. Phantom White Horse 17
4. Tilly and the Cattle Guard 23
5. The Scary Red Devils 27
6. Marooned in the Devils' Kitchen 31
7. What the Wild Goose Knows 37
8. Rebel Hound Dogs 43
9. The Motorcycle Escape 51
10. The Hummingbird 57
11. Forest Ranch - The Fourth Stop 61
12. Side Story: Beautiful Bess 71
13. Side Story: The Swimming Pool 73
14. Side Story: Clint and the Bodybuilder 74
15. Side Story: Rainbow Island 75
16. Side Story: Tilly Come Home 77
17. Side Story: Chickens and Sweet peas 78
18. Side story to side story 79
19. Side Story: The Trophy or What is Falling? 80
20. Meet Me at the Gate 82
21. Just a Boy 83
22. The Truth 84
23. Life's Inviting Trails 86

About the Author-Artist 87

Adventures in Chico and Forest Ranch

STARTING IN ABOUT 1940-TO-1983 OR SO

Introduction

ADVENTURES IN CHICO AND FOREST RANCH

About my stories and the characters in my stories: I write about real people and real places. I haven't changed the names and the dates are as close as I can remember. The stories are absolutely TRUE but please allow for some *slight* exaggerations here and there.

There were five of us in my family. It's Mom Hazel, Dad Wesley Anderson and us the three kids. I (Wilma) was the youngest, loudest and the most excitable. Barbara was a year and a half older than me. She is very fussy, and liked everything clean and pretty. Clinton was the oldest and older by a year. He was the most daring, always into trouble and liked to tease everyone. Our family came to Chico in 1940 or so. When we moved out in the sticks, in 1944 or so, that eastern area of town was called Pleasant Valley. It was mostly open fields of grasshoppers, meadowlarks, and jackrabbits. Our house was the only house on the left side of Cactus Ave while the end of East Ave was a rough, narrow *gravel* road.

Dad used our only vehicle like a work truck. It was a 1932, two-door blue V-8 Ford. He took out the whole back seat and put his plumbing tools in through the trunk every Monday morning before he went to work. So twice a day, we kids had to walk the two or so miles to school located on North and East Ave. Our friend La Donna, who shared in many of our adventures, lived on Mariposa Ave. She often joined us on our way to school. La Donna and I were two girls who love horse riding and adventure.

All four of us kids went to the Pleasant Valley Grammar School. I was in the 5th grade, La Donna and Clint were in the 8th, and Barbara was in the 7th. After school and on weekends, La Donna and I often rode together on our horses.

About the School: in 1944 or so when we arrived, the Pleasant Valley School was in large tall building with a partition divider. Fourth grade was on the west end of the building, and the 5th to 8th grades were on the east side. The wall like divider was only removed on special occasions likes the Christmas play. The school had two teachers for the whole school. The playground equipment consisted of only one tall swing with two seats and some climbing bars but lots of room to run and play. We played speedball, baseball, jump rope, dodge ball and tag, and just ran around.

Wilma (me): I was a tall, dark haired, pigtailed girl and I wanted to be a horse trainer when I grew up. I had received my horse Buck on my eighth birthday. With very little instructions, I began riding him all over Chico. As I look back on some of my adventures, it is surprising that I survived it all.

Buck, he was my little mustang, buckskin, pigeon-toed gelding, and my pride and joy. Bucky, as I called him, was very hard to catch and some days I couldn't catch him at all, even with a pan of oats. I learned to trick him by just sitting down on the field (while listening to the Doves and Meadowlarks) and playing like I didn't want him. If I caught him, often he wouldn't let me put the bridle on, so more tricks were needed.

Then mounting him had to be very fast because if you were slow, you will be bitten at the rear end. He loved to run and was able to run so fast I never lost a bet in a horse race challenge. I always rode bareback and seldom fell off. He was very spooky and excitable, and he hated anything that rattled. Although I pet, brushed, washed and fed him, etc., he never showed me any affection. But he was my *first* horse and I loved him very much.

La Donnas' horse Tilly was a small black thoroughbred type mare, she had two hind white socks with a blaze face, and a very smooth gait that was called a "Single-foot". She was a sweet natured and ready to go horse but often when we were riding, she loved to squeal and kick at Buck. She usually got one of my shins instead.

If my work was done, I was free to ride anywhere and anytime I wished. All that my parents asked of me was I *must* be home before dark.

INTRODUCTION

That left a lot of room for fun and adventure in and around Chico, because behind every good story is a life well lived.

Wilma R. Forester
To my Sister Barbara, who shares my stories.
Love always.
Wilma (Willie)

The Missing Nickel

ADVENTURES IN CHICO
BY WILMA R. FORESTER

Ker-plop ker-plop was the rhythmic sound of little brown sandals alongside the busy road. The long-legged slightly pigeon toed six year old girl was breathing deeply. She had never walked this far alone. After looking both ways for several times, she gathered up her plaid cotton skirt and hurried across busy Nord Ave. in Chico, CA. Mom made all of her dresses and skirts (girls did not wear pants to school in 1940), and they were always too large so she could wear them longer and when they finally fit they were already worn out.

Her mind went back to this morning at Citrus School. She was in the first grade class of Miss Armstrong, who was a long nosed teacher that rode a bike to school. Wilma Rae Anderson wondered if they had missed her yet. Each beat of her heart said, "This is wrong, you'll be in deep trouble!" But how could she go back when the bell had already rung? She could still visualize the face of the large red-haired woman in the white apron looking down at her and repeating several times, "Move on little girl. I gave you your nickel, just move on little girl!"

"No madam, you didn't." I said softly and shyly. "I don't have it." But I obediently moved along and sat down on a bench all by myself and ate my cafeteria lunch. It cost twenty cents. Mom (Hazel) always gave each of us three kids a quarter and a nickel change for us to buy a chocolate covered ice-cream bar with creamy vanilla inside and nuts on top of the chocolate. It was oh so yummy after eating lunch. No one seemed to notice that I was VERY unhappy, near tears and sitting all by myself.

My brother Clinton 9, sister Barbara 8, and I the youngest, lived on West Sacramento Ave. Along with our mom and dad, and our much loved, short legged long haired dog Boogie. It was a modest little home with a big garden and our own cow. We had recently moved here from Los Angeles. My daddy (Wesley, nicknamed Andy) drove a bread truck for Old Home Bread Co. It was located on Park Ave. in Chico. Sometimes in the summer, I got to go with him on his bread route and deliver fresh bread. It smelled so good even a whole block away. We traveled to several of the small towns around Chico as well as nearly every grocery market in town. The truck was so big he had to help me up onto the cool black leather seats, and we would leave before the sun was up. Even today, I still love trucks.

Everybody loved my dad, and laughed and joked with him in almost every store we went to. It was always a fun trip and he usually bought me a Tootsie Roll and some to go home with for the other kids (they were 5 for a penny).

Even at age six, Chico was an awesome wonder to me. How could there be such beautiful streams running through the middle of a town, and people riding horses on a dirt path right down the busy part of a tree lined six lane road? There were trees everywhere and many formed overhead canopies full of fluffy grey squirrels. The one-mile swimming area was almost heaven. It was the largest pool I had ever seen, and it had sweet fresh smelling water running over a fascinating little dam. Then there were thick green toe-tickling lawns everywhere, with woodpeckers and flickers in nearly every one of the huge trees, also fish, lizards, and even pollywogs. On the weekends, the pool was crowded with almost all the kids in Chico plus many of the handsome young soldiers from the Chico Airport. These young men were stationed in tent- like barracks, hundreds and hundreds of them. My family and most of Chico would drive out to the Airport every Fourth of July and Memorial Day to watch them in grand musical celebrations and parades. But I was more interested in the pollywogs.

I walked fast as I was passing the little shops and open market stores on Nord Ave., almost running and thinking hard, is this the right way home? Then I remembered mom often made a right hand turn from Nord onto Sacramento Ave. right where I was. She would hold her arm out the window to signal, while she was driving our blue 1936 Ford V-Eight. I think it was right there. What if I went the wrong way? I do not want to go back to school. It was too late and maybe I couldn't find the way back anyway. Where would I end up when it gets dark and if I will make it home, would Mom be glad to see me or angry? I began to think this wasn't very smart of me. She might be VERY angry! But I felt so cheated, oh how I wanted that NICKEL. All the other kids got their ice cream bar but I didn't get mine!

I passed by lots of people working out in their beautiful flower filled yards. They didn't seem to notice me. Didn't they know I shouldn't be here? A few dogs ran out barking and startled me but thankfully they stayed in their yards. Suddenly, there down the road on the right side of West Sacramento Ave., I could see the reddish brown roof of our house peeking through the tall magnificent black walnut trees that lined the driveway. There was our dog Boogie, running out to greet me but I didn't feel like petting him right now. I rushed up to the front steps and pushing open the screen door, I rushed in and stood there in the middle of the front room a little breathless with my knees slightly unsteady. Mom turned from the kitchen sink with an open mouthed stare of surprise at the sight of me.

"Willie, what are you doing home and how did you get here?!" She demanded. I had not planned out exactly what to say and now, there were no words just tears. She didn't spank me! Drying her hands she sat me on her lap until I finally sobbed out the whole story. When I finished, the red- haired cafeteria lady sounded like the wicked witch in the Snow-White movie.

Mom wiped my tears away and carefully explained that what I had done was very wrong and very dangerous, and I must NEVER do it again. We had no phone to call the school, so after I got a nickel in my sweaty little palm, we went back to Citrus School in a hurry. First, we went to the Ice Cream place, (I was so glad it was still open) and I gave the lady my new nickel. I felt relieved that it was a different lady. At last, I got to eat my chocolate covered ice-cream bar, then off to my class room. Wow, the teacher was embarrassed because I hadn't even been missed yet. Mom explained the events of the afternoon to Miss Armstrong, who was beginning to frown down her long nose at me and then they both lectured me some more, while all the other kids looked on. How embarrassing, I felt my face turning rosy red.

Finally when mom left and the classroom calmed down, I got seated at my desk and started to work on my spelling lesson. I reached inside the special tiny pocket mom had sewn into my too big skirt searching for my short yellow pencil. There was NO pencil but my fat little fingers closed on a NICKEL

The Treasured Dungeon

ADVENTURES IN CHICO
BY WILMA R. FORESTER

"Come on Barbs, let's take a shortcut by this old building." I was running ahead of my sister and ducking under some small bushes.

"Oh look Willie, there is a stairway on the back of this place!" said Barbara. We had noticed a closed sign hanging by one nail on the front of the building. The stairs were rickety, dusty and spread with cob webs. With a big smile, she waved her hands and said, "I am going to live in a house with stairs when I grow up!"

It was Saturday morning and we were walking along Nord Ave. on the way to the Senator Theater for the matinee show. We lived several miles down West Sacramento Ave., close to the Borges Dairy and Mom always gave us each a quarter for the show on Saturday.

As we cautiously climbed up the stairs and pushed on the door, it was ajar and we peeked in, and began to explore the dusty mostly empty rooms. We started giggling at the excitement of running from room to room just looking around. Then Barbara finally followed me into the last back room.

"Willie where are you? You disappeared?' She called. "I am down here," came my faint answer. As I went into the last room, I saw a trap door built into the floor. I pried it open and when I peeked down into dark areas below I saw - TREASURES! Treasures covered in dust and spider webs but shelves and tables piled and stacked with candy, tools, bread, cookies, canned goods, jars of honey, dog food, toys and more. With great excitement, I dropped down onto the top shelf of Treasures.

"Oh Barbs, I found everything our family will ever need. Mom and Dad won't ever have to work again!" I called up to her. I thought of Dad and his back problems, and how he was sometimes out of work because of it. She did NOT understand.

"Willie, you get out of there before the police come!" She yelled.

Why oh, why do big sisters have to ruin everything? I thought to myself.

"They will take you away and put you in jail for the rest of your life!" She shouted down at me. I ignored her, and found more and more things, like

Hostess Twinkies, etc. When I glanced up at the trap door again I considered HOW will I get out of here? Then my imagination kicked in and I could visualize a big burly cop standing there glaring down at me. He had a gold badge and a big billy club. With his hands on his hips, he demanded, "Little girl, what are you doing down there?"

"Willie, I am going to tell on you! You get out of there!" Maybe she was right. So, I climbed back onto the top shelf and tried to climb out but I couldn't get a hold of the edge. I started getting scared. How to get back out of this spooky place? Think Willie, don't panic, think. I climbed back down and started stacking cans of food and boxes on top of the shelf. Then with shaking knees, I carefully climbed up on the top of the pile and I could just reach the edge but I still couldn't quite make it out. Then Barbs got a hold of my shirt and pulled hard. I skinned my knee a bit but I MADE it out! We quickly tiptoed through the dusty rooms and down the back stairs, and on to the matinee show. Dad picked us up as usual and drove us home after the show. His back was much better. Later that night, Mom asked how I skinned my knee? I didn't answer, I just got real busy drying the dishes. Barbara looked up at me but she didn't say a word. I didn't even get one little piece of all that candy and she wouldn't help me with the dishes either.

On our next trip to the show, we crossed the street and we never walked on that side of Nord Ave. again. We found out later that it was an old closed grocery store with an empty apartment on top and there was a skylight between them. What was my "Treasured Dungeon" is now a Pizza Parlor on Nord Ave. in Chico several years later.

P.S. Barbara now lives in a beautiful house with a stairway! And so do I!

Phantom White Horse

ADVENTURES IN CHICO
BY WILMA R. FORESTER

"See those hills with that little green valley up to the right side of the Park? Well, I am going to tell all a story about a phantom snow white horse that may still be up there for all ah know," said our new neighbor to us. It was about 1942 and the Anderson family had moved to Pleasant Valley. The street was called Cactus Ave. for some reason. It was way out in the sticks at that time in the northeast part of Chico. There were five of us plus a dog, a cat and one cow. The family consisted of my father, Wesley (Andy), mother Hazel, brother Clinton (12), sister Barbara (11) and I Wilma or Willie (9). Our house was the only house on the short gravel road, except for a small place across the road on the far end where Mr. Walker and his family lived East Ave. which was also a narrow gravel lane that dead-ended on Cactus. To continue, going east you made a sharp right and then on to Manzanita Ave. which lead towards upper Bidwell Park. Me and my siblings attended Pleasant Valley School that was located at John A. McManus Ave. Our new school was a large one-roomed building with a partition divider and had all the grades up to the eighth.

Elderly Mister Walker continued his tale. "I told this before, there's this white horse up that valley and he's nearly blind. He is a part Arab bred horse. He was put up there because they couldn't ride him that much. They said he was too old, so he got turned loose up in that green valley right yonder beyond those green trees." Mr. Walker waves his arm and gestures as he talks. "He scares people because he'll walk right up to yah. So they call him The Phantom." That was all I needed to hear. I was too shy to ask any questions but my imagination went wild. I loved horses and a beautiful Arabian horse. It must be a stallion, with a long white flowing mane and tail, running free and wild up in that green valley. It was an irresistible, glorious, wonderfully attractive picture that Mr. Walker put in a little girl's mind. Nearly every day as I walked the two miles to and from school, I looked up into those foothills and that horse was all I could think of. I pictured myself befriending and catching this magnificent animal, leading it home (maybe even riding it) and then galloping around the school with his mane and my pigtails flowing in the wind, showing off to all my friends.

So one fine Saturday morning, after I had bugged everyone for months with my dreams, we three kids climbed through the barbed wire fence where East Ave. ended (that was our shortcut to the upper park and green tree area to the left of the park), and started another one of many wild adventures. Clint was in the lead with his trusty B-B gun to protect his two little sisters. He was the bolder one but also the easiest one to get spooked. Barbara was the fussy slow one (she didn't want to get her white tennis shoes dirty) and I was the impulsive excitable one, usually in the middle but sometimes needing help just to tie my shoes. This day I wore my cowboy boots and I had tucked a short tie rope plus an apple in my back pocket, I was ready to catch that Phantom White Horse.

Because of the recent spring rains which made our feet sink into the mud with nearly every step, it was very slow movement. Barbara soon started to complain and even wanted to go back. After an hour of trudging around little pools and spring flowers, we seemed to be no closer to the hills. Then our beloved Brownie, the ugliest, dumbest dog in the world, spotted a Jack rabbit and off he went at top speed yelping and disappeared out of sight.

I need to tell you a little side story here about how we got Brownie. A friend of our dad had a beautiful silky black and white bird dog who had pups. She surprised everyone and had nine of them. Daddy said we could have one puppy. So the whole family went to pick out our new dog. There were black and white, brown and white, all black, all white, some with long hair, some with short hair, several soft and silky ones like the mother dog, and the last one was a brown potbellied runt with a pig like nose, yellow eyes and a rat tail. "Well kids, which one do you want?" Asked the man. "You get to pick from the whole litter?"

"Oh daddy," I said, grabbing up a fat silky black and white one, "We want this one."

"No daddy," Barbara declared, "We want this beautiful fluffy brown and white one."

Clint would not be outdone. While covering his mouth to keep from laughing out loud, he announced, "I want the brown one!"

Mom and Dad always thought Clint could do no wrong and in spite of the tears of "the girls", they agreed we should get the brown one. No one could think of a name for IT so we just called him Brownie. (He lived 18 years or more.)

Passing just a little left of the white Easter Cross in the park, we stopped to examine it with great respect. We all three went to the local church and loved what the real Easter Celebration stood for. We continued along the power line road almost running with excitement, loving our time of adventure and freedom up in the beautiful Sierra Nevada foothills. The open grassy plains were all covered with flowers, mostly scrambled eggs flowers but also with buttercups, and lupines were sprinkled here and there with spots of white meadowfoam.

Still no Brownie in sight but a nice gravelly road leads us to the sides of a strand of live oak trees sprinkled with tall pines and on beyond were the green valleys. A little stream swirled across and over the road which had turned to hard lava bedrock for the most part. Clint got to the stream first and was trying to cross it. Then he sat down on a rock and waited for us girls to catch up. It was a breathtaking spot with a small waterfall plunging into a little canyon below us and a magnificent view of the whole city of Chico, the Chico Airport plus the Coast Range Mts.

"Oh look! There is our little old house down there on Cactus Ave." We were laughing and talking loudly, all seated on rocks near the water. Even dumb Brownie showed up and was panting and lying in the now muddy water.

"Come on Barbs and Willie," he called us. "Let's go!" Clint yelled.

"Wait Clint, I can't. Something is wrong with my heart. I am shaking clear down to my boots." I said.

"Me too!" yelled Barbs.

"Wow!" said Clint, feeling the rocks beneath us. "What is happening to us? Somebody must be drilling a well right here behind these trees."

With eyes wide in wonder, we all started to search for the source of the heavy bone jarring, rhythmic pounding. To this day, we still talk about it and we never found an answer to this puzzle. There was no one drilling anywhere. When we explored the waterfall and pool in the lava rocks below it, there was no reason for it, nothing. The pounding sound centered only on that one spot where the water crossed the road. It is still a complete MYSTERY to us!

The search for the Phantom Horse must go on, so up the road we went. The trees were taller and thicker now with darker shadows everywhere, the grass was higher and Clint was getting spooked.

"Willie, how do you know this is the way to go? What did Mr. Walker say? I think he is full of baloney anyway!" continued Clint. We were walking slower and bunched up closer together now. Clint was still in the lead with his B-B gun on a full ready 10 pumps. We had come too far to turn back now! Our eyes searched every little hill and valley as we peeked beneath some of the bigger oak trees limbs and beat about the taller bushes, there was not a sound now just the wheeeee of the wind blowing.

No Phantom White Horse! Not even hoof prints! Suddenly dumb Brownie started barking loudly! He was jumping and running in and out of the tall brush and poison oak. We all three whirled around and ran as fast as we could, all the way back to where the mystery pounding had been. As we stopped to listen again for the booming sound, catch our breath and calm our hearts, surprisingly it was quiet, just the trickling sound of the waterfall and some doves calling in the distance.

Back down the gravel road for home, we went. A little tired and (I especially) very disappointed we started to climb back through the hole in the barbed wire fence and then here came Brownie. He smelled real bad and he had something in his mouth as well. He had been rolling in what looked like horse manure! Looking back up toward the green valley, I was thinking, just maybe there was a real White Horse up there. Oh well, Clint seemed relieved when he helped us crawl back through the wire fence and Barbara's white tennis shoes were speckled with red brown mud, so I would have to let my "Phantom White Horse" fantasy go for now. At least I had an apple to eat on the rest of the way home.

P.S. I didn't really hate Brownie. I just petted him only when no one else was looking.

Tilly and the Cattle Guard

ADVENTURES IN CHICO 1944
BY WILMA R. FORESTER

Tilly and the Cattle Guard

Tilly backed and snorted softly, tucking her black tail down tight, she shook her head sideways as if saying no, noo NOOO! She was a beautiful thoroughbred mare, small, black and shiny with a smooth single-foot gait to her.

Her rider, my friend, La Donna had just asked her to cross a thing that appeared horrible to her. It was shiny bars of steel with deep spaces of blackness. It was a cattle guard built into the road meant to stop all grazing animals from crossing. If they tried, it meant entrapment and injury, and often to be left for a terrible death.

We were going for a ride in the upper Bidwell Park. Two young girls, I was about eleven and she was perhaps twelve or so. It looked harmless to us because we had never even noticed a cattle guard being there before. Cars drove over it and we wanted to ride our horses in upper Bidwell Park today. (That road is now called Wildwood Ave. and the cattle guard has been removed.)

La Donna casually urged the wide-eyed-mare to get across this thing. It was blocking our way. Tilly put her head down and closely examined this terrible metal apparatus, and then she did the impossible. She stepped onto it very, very carefully with her front feet then placing her hind feet exactly where the front feet had been, she slowly tiptoed all the way across. O.K. she made it so I am next. I whorled my buckskin pony to get him in control and headed him towards this thing (Dad said I had to be the boss). He slammed on the brakes and shook his head. After three or more whorls he began to step back and forth, and I knew he would NOT do it. I called for Donna to wait for me, and I began to look for another way to get on DOWN this road. Sure enough there was a gate off to my left. I slid off and opened it, led Buck through, closed the gate, and grabbing his mane, I slide up in one smooth move and off we went to explore the upper park.

As you can imagine, this was an unbelievable feat of agility for Tilly and it could have resulted in her death and serious injury for her rider as well (Note: No one should ever try that and we SHOULD have known better).

On up to the Five Mile swimming hole (Hooker Oak Pool), we rode. Letting the horses splash in the causeway. We crossed Lindo Channel and continued over to the old famous Hooker Oak tree (said to be the largest in the world). There, we let the horse graze under the tree while we climbed up into the huge twisted limbs. Then after jumping our horses back and forth over the cement enclosure for a while, we rode back along Manzanita Ave. and avoided the cattle guard on our way back home.

When we told where we went and all about our ride, our neighbor Mr. Walker, was visiting there with my dad. He was a retired cattleman, when he heard our story of Tilly crossing the cattle guard, he loudly stated, "I don't believe that. It would be impossible for a horse to do that, I have NEVER heard of such a ridiculous thing!" We both got quiet and never repeated the story again, but we both knew Tilly DID it!

The Scary Red Devils

ADVENTURE IN CHICO
BY WILMA R. FORESTER

"I can't go! My knee is so sore I can't get on my horse!" My friend, La Donna had a boil right on her kneecap and it hurt.

It was spring. Scrambled eggs, buttercup and meadowfoam were spread out like beautiful patchwork sheets all across the open fields in Eastern Chico, and I wanted to go horseback riding. We loved to spend hours and hours riding in Bidwell Park but she wasn't up to it today. Still, I would not leave her alone.

"Donna, I will get the horses all ready and I will even help you get on." I coaxed and coaxed her for half an hour and finally she agreed to go. Today, we rode by Horseshoe Lake and up into the upper park. It had been raining and the creek was too high to cross so we were happy to wade the horses out to a pretty nearby gravel bar. Once there, we decided (she was tired already) to sit in the sun and play in the water a bit. We dug a little pool and tried to trap some small fish. The cliffs behind us were dripping with ferns and flowers. I felt just blessed to be there, it was just a BEAUTIFUL spot.

"EEEEK!" she screamed. "What is that?" She pointed to a weird brown lizard with bulging eyes and a fiery red belly, and then there was another one, and another right behind us. It squirmed around and stuck a red tongue out at us. They were ALL over the place. She started to yell and holler, and I grabbed a rock and threw it at several of them but I could not scare them away! We had never seen such a thing and we both panicked. I grabbed my horse Buck's mane, and I was on and out of there in a flash. I crossed the water and over onto the trail in a split second, I was ready to GET out of there!

But when I looked back, she was still standing there loudly screaming. She and her horse Tilley were surrounded by the scary red devils! I forgot she could not get on because of her sore knee! What to do? I really did not want to go back! But I had talked her into going and I couldn't leave her now. So, back across the water went Buck and I, while trying not to let him step on one of those scary things. What if they bite my horse? I dismounted and while shaking a bit, I put my hand on my bent knee and she painfully stepped up and slid up onto Tilley's back. I quickly remounted Buck, and like two frightened Indians, we both raced out of the scary red devils' encampment.

We gave up on our ride and just went on back home. Now, I am not afraid of most snakes or lizards but I need to know what it is? I found out from my Dad, those were harmless salamanders, "Mud Puppies" they are called. I am so sorry if I hurt any of them that day. They are very common in Northern CA. It is fun to catch and play with them. Just be sure to put them back in the stream and wash your hands when you are done handling them. Salamanders collect in large bunches in the spring for the mating season and I know they meant us no harm.

I learned a lot about salamanders and I learned NOT to coax someone into doing something if they really don't want to DO it. Even if the scary red devils, among other things, ruined our ride that day, we were back riding again by the very next weekend!

Marooned in the Devils' Kitchen

ADVENTURES IN CHICO
BY WILMA R. FORESTER

In about 1945 or so, three girls were skipping and laughing along East Ave which was at that time a narrow gravel road that turned right at Cactus Ave, and joined Manzanita Ave. It was a crisp fall day with Wilma (Willie) 13, and Barbara 14, and La Donna 15. We were out for some good time. We headed into upper Bidwell Park, just kicking leaves collecting oak balls, chasing a baby squirrel etc.

We passed by Horseshoe Lake when a group of horse riders connected with us. It was my Mom, Dad and brother Clint, out riding. "Dad, can you lead my horse home for me? I want to go with the girls," called out Clint.

"OK Clint, but you must all be home by dark," replied my dad. La Donna and Clint were about the same age, and Clint loved to tease her just to watch her blush. So now there were four of us plus our dog Brownie (I called him dumb Brownie, but that is another story).

While laughing and talking, we continued strolling along the upper Park Road for several miles then we saw a park sign that read, "The Devils Kitchen". Wow, we followed the trail and explored the place. Oh, what a neat exciting place it was. We climbed over the large lava rocks and stared up at the sheer wall like cliffs. Our voices echoed through the narrow passages. Many of them opened up into large very tall rooms.

"Wow, what a neat hideout this would make," said Clint.

"I bet the Indians lived in here," said La Donna. Barking, Brownie raced about while checking all of the holes and cracks for varmints. After hiking on down the trail to the creek below, we climbed around to some huge lava boulders and sat high upon the top rocks cautiously peeking down into the dark chambers of The Devils Kitchen below us.

"If we had some food, we could stay all night," stated Clint. He was always hungry. Barbara and La Donna were singing Johnny Cash's new hit, "I'll walk the Line". With all the strange echoes, it sounded like a choir. I was petting Brownie (Dumb Brownie).

It was getting late in the day when La Donna dropped down onto a rock ledge five or six feet below us. "What are you doing Donna? How are you going to get back up?" yelled Clint.

"Well, I see some more ledges below me," she yelled back up, "and I think I can climb clear down to the bottom on these rocks. Come on you guys, it will be fun."

"No way, I am not jumping down there. Besides, we would get our pants all dirty," said Barbara.

Donna, who was out of our sight by now, continued her climbing and jumping, and surprisingly she made it all the way down to the rocky bottom. "Come on you guys!" She continued to holler back up toward us. Barbara and I stood staring down just not convinced about jumping onto that ledge below us.

Clint said, "No way with these cowboy boots on. I would NOT make it."

After a while Donna walked out from the bottom and around to the top again. "Oh, come on, I'll show you how to do it." She was wearing her Indian moccasins and shorts, and she laughed and gracefully jumped down there again.

"OK," said Barbs. "If she can do it, we can! Come on Willie!" The jump was so far you had to get a run at it, but we both made it down onto the huge, rough lava rock beside La Donna.

Strangely, she sat there looking over the edge and said, "Just look how far I would fall." She kicked a small rock off and we watched it falling, ring, ping, pang, clang, clear down to about forty feet or more, landing on the jagged rocky floor.

"Well, show us how to get down," Barbara said.

After a long pause, she wiped her eyes and said, "I can't, I hurt my foot this time."

Fear is infectious and we all three caught it at once. We sat there staring down at the rocks on the bottom while crying loud boohoos. There stood Clint and Brownie looking down at three bawling girls huddled on a rock. To add to our misery, the sun dipped behind a cloud. It was getting dark, turning cold and the wind whipped the top of the rocks blowing grit in our eyes. "What are we going to do now?"

Then Clint disappeared from view. Oh dear, had he gone for help? He was very afraid of the dark. Had he left us? But he re-appeared after about half an hour with a bunch of brush and grass which he tossed down to us plus his coat for us to sit on. Several hours later, the moon pecked out and the cold wind whipped up even stronger. We could hear animal sounds around, and below us down in the devil's room underneath us. We shivered and huddled together even more. I began to picture a sad Mom and Dad finding three dead bodies on top of this rock weeks from now or maybe just three skeletons. I began to pray a lot, but as I glanced up at the moon with clouds drifting all around it, I imagined seeing the face of the devil himself standing just below the clouds. Because he was in his kitchen, he was holding a cooking fork instead of a pitchfork and wearing an apron while he laughed down at us. How could this have happened? The wind died down and the night finally got very quiet and all five of us just sat there. Nobody knew WHAT to do! We were marooned in the Devil's Kitchen!

Suddenly Brownie started barking wildly. There was a car coming! We could see the glow of headlights bouncing off the big oak trees branches. Someone was driving down from further up the road. It was quite a distance away, but Clint jumped up and started to run as fast as he could go, back down the trail we came. But it was too dark and too far, and he couldn't intercept them. But Brownie COULD and did!

"What is that barking, yelping dog doing way up here this time of night?" The three fishermen asked each other, then they stopped the truck.

"Help, help! We need help!" yelled a breathless Clint.

Help we got! They had ropes and a flashlight among the usual pile of tools in a fisherman's pickup. One man jumped down onto our rock and tied a rope around us, and the other two men pulled us up one by one. La Donna lost a shoe and had to be carried to the truck. Two of the men plus Clint and of course Brownie rode in the truck bed, and we three shivering girls piled in front with a coat over us. After several miles of traveling slowly along the upper park road, we met my Dad in his Ford V-8. He had searched nearly all of Bidwell Park, and Dad had firmly reminded us to be home before dark, but he was so happy to find us he forgot to be angry. We had narrowly escaped being marooned in the Devil's Kitchen!

Brownie, well maybe he wasn't so dumb after all? But that is another story.

What the Wild Goose Knows

ADVENTURES IN CHICO (1945)
BY WILMA R. FORESTER

I looked up at my Mom and ask if it would live? Then to my Dad, "Can you fix it Daddy?" I had already said a quiet prayer. In my head I was hearing the song.

My Heart knows what the wild goose knows and I must go where the wild goose goes. Wild goose, brother goose which is best a wandering soul or a heart at rest? Let it fly! Let it fly! Let it fly! I could even hear the lonely French horns calling out in the song.

In the winter, our home on Cactus Ave, was surrounded by shallow ponds and runoff streams. This was attractive to waterfowl. This winter was an exceptionally wet one but spring was just around the corner.

It was a foggy evening and large flocks of goose had been flying over all day. My brother Clinton (about 13) was afraid of the dark so I (about 11) went out with him to milk our cow, Betty Lou. As we came back into the house (the only house on the left side of Cactus Ave), a large group of birds passed overhead. They honked loudly and chattered to each other as they headed north. The sound was loud as they flew steadily on, and then became a weak and very slow honk! One bird was way behind the flock and flying very low. Bang! Whap! Flop! Then silence.

Clint jumped up and said, "Come on Willie, we have to see what that was!" We still had our coats so he grab the flashlight and we ran out the back door to see what that sound was. He yelled to Mom, "Don't let Brownie (our dog) out until we get back!"

It was so foggy, we bumped into each other as we felt our way along the gravel road trying to guess where that sound came from. When he shined the light toward the bottom of the telephone pole along our road, there was something in the weeds. We approached slowly and carefully but it doesn't move. He knew it had to be one of the birds that had just passed overhead. Clint handed me the flashlight, and whipping off his coat, he gathered what looked like a dirty pile of feathers into a bundle and we carried it together into the house. He opened his coat onto the kitchen table and out fell a beautiful bird. The whole family gathered around to stare at it. Then Mom said, "Too bad it didn't drop in to our Christmas dinner." How could she think like that, I wanted that bird to be alive!

Dad spread out the wings and one was a bit twisted with several broken feathers and all stained with blood. After we all stared at it quietly for awhile Mom said to me, "Willie, go get me the masking tape!"

Dad said, "Clint, go get me that cardboard box on the back porch!"

Mom carefully taped the injured wing into a more normal position, up close to the body of the limp bird. Then Dad gently placed it in the box and covered the box with a towel. The black eyes of the bird seemed to be looking at me. We sat the box out on the screened in back porch.

"Let's see if it is alive in the morning," Dad said.

We tried looking it up in our "Book of Knowledge" but we were still not sure exactly what kind of bird it was. We all agreed it must be a grey goose.

In the morning, I was the first one to check on the goose. It was alive and standing up.

Dad said, "Let's put it in the chicken pen because that would be the only safe place for a helpless bird." We did.

Of course the next day, I had to go to school but when I returned "Goose Gander" as we called him, was up and eating grain and grass with the chickens. The poor rooster was quite alarmed at such a large intruder. Several days later as the weather improved, Mom let the chickens out as usual to scratch and wander in the cow pasture and Goose went with them. I watched closely to see if he would return and go to bed with them that night. He did, but he slept in the corner on the ground with his head under his good wing. So he continued to be a part of our yard full of chickens. He didn't like Brownie. He stayed as far away as he could from us as well as the dog. He would cock his head to one side as he watched us. I often thought to myself, what a sad looking misfit. He liked to play in the usually muddy winter ponds and eventually the tape wore off but the injured wing was still short of a few feathers and a bit twisted, and I never heard him honk?

Summer came and went. One evening when Clint was out milking Betty Lou he called, "Hey Willie, Goose Gander just flew around the barn." I ran out just in time to see him land back near the chickens.

"I am afraid he won't ever be a wild goose again," stated mom. "I think he is permanently injured and he had been with the chickens so long, he thinks he is a chicken." I knew what she was really thinking, "Christmas is coming and we have been feeding this bird too long."

The fall rains came and with it several flocks of geese passed near our place. Goose flapped his wings and honked a few times but he stayed on the ground with the chickens.

There is something wonderful and magical about wild waterfowl. They know when and where to fly, and they often travel thousands of miles to far away mysterious lands. God must have given them more than just normal bird instincts to do what they do! I was sad to think this one might never fly again.

After several months, winter had passed and spring wasn't too far away. One beautiful evening, the clouds had just parted when a large flock of wild ones passed over our little house. They were heading north. They were honking and calling like children, all talking at once. Goose flapped his wings, and got all excited calling and honking to them. But he was too late. They were moving on. Then something completely unexpected happened. Three or four of the birds circled back over the house flying low and calling loudly. They had heard him, maybe they even knew him! Goose flapped his wings and running as fast as he could go across the rough ground, he rose up and cleared the barn and then slowly circled back over the house flying quite low. Maybe he was saying goodbye to the chickens but I prefer to think he was saying THANK YOU to us. He gracefully raised gaining speed as he went. The larger group circled clear back around and then the smaller group with Goose Gander in among them, joined with them. The whole group together circled overhead once more and then he was GONE!

My heart knows what the wild goose knows and I must go where the wild goose goes, wild goose, brother goose which is best a wandering fool or a heart at rest? Let it fly! Let it fly! Let it fly away! Listen for the lonely sound of the French horns.

We never saw him again! But when the wild ones fly over every spring, you will see me looking up and searching the sky for one big white bird with dark eyes and a slightly twisted wing.

Oh yes, one more BIG surprise. We finally found his picture in our "Book of Knowledge", and Goose Gander was not a goose. He was really a Trumpeter Swan.

Rebel Hound Dogs

ADVENTURES IN CHICO, CA
BY WILMA R. FORESTER

Rebel Hound Dogs

A buzzing sounded in the middle of the trail.

"Here hold my horse," said Callie. "I am going to kill that thing!" I did and she did.

We had an all planned terrific, exciting overnight ride, and we were on our way. As I watched her get a big stick and whack the rattlesnake (we normally just rode around them but this one was on a narrow uphill trail), I thought back to the first time I met her.

Picture this. A racing away golden Palomino horse with its long white mane and tail trailing out behind. Clinging to the saddle was a beautiful girl hanging on for dear life. Her long brunette was flying behind her as was her jacket, sleeping bag, and other things she had carefully packed on the saddle. She was not screaming as I would have been. The horse, Pal, had come from behind the other riders, every man perhaps thirty or so raced along the left side of the fence in upper Bell Park. Every man (all cowboys) would cut over and attempt to ward her off. Pal just charged along faster and outrun every one of them. He finally ran out of air up near the Easter Cross. She reached out and got a hold of the reins which had flipped over his head and started the whole thing. It was the Annual Sheriff Posse Ride and Bandit Chase, happening in beautiful Bidwell Park.

The three bandits had already taken off to hide from all of the other riders. I watched her ride back gathering all her things along the way. I figured she would have a good cry and go on back home. But she laughed and rejoined the group. It was a wonderful overnight ride, about twenty miles up and past the end of the park to the Mickey Ranch. By car it was up Hwy. 32 and down below Forest Ranch to Chico creek. There was a nice dinner waiting for us with a place to camp all set up. I even caught a Bandit, and received a twenty-five dollar reward. However the best thing I received on that ride was a new friendship with a terrific young girl, named Callie. How she came in Chico is another side story but I will save that one for later.

Back to my story: After she wacked the rattlesnake, she remounted and we continued on our trip. It was already late in the day and we had a looong way

45

to go. We had spent the last day or so cleaning out an old abandoned cabin to make this ride happen. We had driven up Hwy. 32 to the Fourteen Mile House and down that road almost to the creek, with boards, nails, a hammer, etc. We managed to clean the cabin, fix the corral for our horses and make it ready for our overnight stay. Years ago, it had been a nice ranch house with a nice barn but now there were no doors or windows in the cabin and the barn was almost flat. Note: O.J. Simons, the owner, had given us permission to do this.

We found fruit trees and a fig tree with ripe figs too. The rickety walkway to the cabin crossed a cold spring full of lush watercress. It was very enjoyable cleaning, fixing and exploring everything. Now it was all ready for us and we were on our way, riding up from Cactus Ave. in Chico.

I was riding my Royal Red Bud, quarter horse. I called him Buddy. He was chestnut colored with white stocking feet behind, and a star and snip on his face. I have had several horses that were very dear to me, but if I had to pick just one, it would be Buddy. That horse truly loved me. I could trust him anywhere, anytime. He always tried his best to please me. He was almost like a big loving dog in horsehide plus being powerful, smooth and terrific to ride.

We rode to the end of the Park through the broken fence and then on some more. By the time we found a place to cross the creek and located the road up to the cabin, it was getting dark. Trudging up the mountain we arrived just in time to feed and care for the horses, fix dinner, which was cold hotdogs, with potato salad, (we added watercress of course). It was fall so we decided not to have a fire. It would be too dangerous. Our beds were already made on the cabin floor right near the open window. It was completely dark when we finally crawled in. We lay there talking and laughing for a while. She recounted how she came to Chico when she was 13 years old.

Now here is THAT story: Yvonne Bundy (the name Callie came later) lived in Seattle Washington, with her younger brother Ted. Their bedroom was in the cellar of the house. Mom and Dad had a drinking problem, and were emotionally and physically abusive to the two children. The only thing she had beside her brother that she really cared about was a grey cat. She saved her money and bought an old used Motor Scooter. Taking a few clothes and her cat, she put everything in a cardboard box, which she tied on the back of the Scooter, and on a dark rainy day, she headed out as far as a tank of gas would take her and that was Chico, CA. A kindly lady named Mrs. Mac Fall took them in. Callie told me later, I must go back for my brother Ted, he is sooo miserable living there, but she never went back. She felt so strongly about having NO connection to her parents that she legally changed her name to Callie De Monte.

I know, I know Ted Bundy from Washington?!? I thought about that possible connection years later, but when I checked it out they said, "Ted Bundy didn't have a sister?" But they looked SO very much alike. Maybe she left before they knew about his sister?

Meanwhile, we had retired to our nice bed back in the old cabin. Calm Callie went right to sleep but I, being a more nervous type, lay awake and listened to all the night sounds. I felt something (small) jump on my blankets so I searched around in the dark for the little flashlight but couldn't find it. Then I finally drifted off to sleep. But I woke several hours later with a very faint sound of I am not sure what? As I drifted in and out of sleep the sound came and went but it was defiantly getting closer. Finally I nudged Callie, "Do you hear that? What could that be in the middle of the night? I mean we are up here on this mountainside in the wilderness so what do you think that is?"

She listened a while, "I think it might be hound dogs baying." She continued, "Well, I knew a dog trainer that ran and trained his dogs at night because that is when the raccoons are out but they probably won't come way up here unless they are on the wrong trail. Besides the raccoons are usually down by the creek, so go back to sleep, O.K.?"

I tried but again they woke me and they were defiantly closer this time. I nudged her awake again, and this time we both sat up and listened out the open window. No one knew we were here in this old abandoned cabin. The horses were up the hill, out of sight and we had no lights or car. Maybe they are trailing us? The moon was up by now and the loud baying of a whole pack of hounds was coming closer and closer to our little cabin. As we sat there staring out the window, we were very much AWAKE by now!

Suddenly, they all broke through the brush at once. Rough talking men, I never knew exactly how many there were, they were carrying rifles with at least six hound dogs baying and barking loud and excited! The dogs ran right towards the cabin!

"Hey you dumb mute dawgs, gat away from thet cabin winder!" There came a very loud gruff male voice.

"Let's take a break right here," said another. They leaned against the cabin wall and slid down by our window leaving their guns sticking up in the air. They were out of breath, talking loud and rough while coughing and blowing. I have heard a lot of curse words in my life but that day I learned a few more. Soon, one was puffing on a pipe and the other lit a cigar. Of course the smoke came right in our open window. There, we sat just inches from them, bolt upright and wearing our skimpy underwear (it was a warm night). I felt like my hair was standing bolt upright also.

The gruff voices continued, "Hey do yah member ole blue there? Well I thought I was rid of him, he turned rebel on me yah know. He went ta chasing abbets. I wacked them with my gun, I did. He ran off but by--------- he came back and I am still a trying to teach them something. Rebels will get after anything! I hate trying to learn a --------------Rebel dawg anything and that one IS a rebel!

Then one dog put his nose in through our window and he looked right at us! He stuck his front feet up on the window sill while he wagged his tail. Soon another joined him. They began to take turns looking in at us sitting there. Their big brown eyes said, "Would you please pet me?" I could have reached them but we were both still frozen in fear and shock.

"Ole Blue GIT yourself out of that winder," yelled one of them! "What is wrong with them dawgs?" He continued. "Do yah think that meth be a--- varmint in that there cabin?"

"Naw, them dawgs would be a barking if there war." They sat there quite a while telling more dog stories and smoking and spiting, etc.

After what seemed like a looonng time, Callie started feeling for our tiny little flashlight and then she found it under the blanket edge and quietly stuck it in my hand.

What was I supposed to do? Stand up in my underwear and shine it right at them and demand that they leave? I just might get shot! But I flipped it on anyway and oh my gosh, I dropped it at the same time! It flashed a light up on the ceiling and then rolled out the door into the watercress and slowly dropped under the boards of the spring making a very strange glow in the sky. Suddenly everything got REAL QUITE!

Finally one of the men said, "What was that?" More quiet, then, "I don't know," said a very soft voice, "but I am getting OUT ta here! This ole place is too spooky for me!" They called and whistled for their rebel hound dogs and soon back through the bushes zipped all of them. We sat there and listened to the fading sounds of the hounds, which were baying again, until it all got quiet and disappeared. Callie went right back to sleep and I finally fell asleep just before morning came.

The next day after we cleaned, gathered everything and saddled up, it was warm already, so we stopped for a fun skinny dip swim in the creek below the cabin. Then off for a great ride back toward Chico we went. Later when we arrived at home, my neighbor asked, "Did you have any fun or adventures on your ride?"

I said, "You wouldn't believe it," and she wouldn't have either. Later I went to town and bought myself a new flashlight, a BIG one!

P.S. The last time I saw Callie, she and her son were on their way to Alaska to raise and train husky sled dogs. That was many years ago and sadly, I haven't heard from her since. I truly hope her brother didn't turn out to be the Notorious Ted Bundy Serial Killer. Whether or not, what a fun, brave, and adventuresome gal she was, however just like me, I think she too was just a bit of a rebel.

The Motorcycle Escape

ADVENTURES IN FOREST RANCH
BY WILMA R. FORESTER

"Quick Marge, hold up this wire fence! I think I can slide my motorcycle under it! We need to get out of here NOW!" I shouted.

The morning started with us just riding around. We were still looking for that strange cave someone had told us about. It was said to be somewhere close in Forest Ranch, so we would try different paths or trails here and there but so far no cave.

Most of the time, we were both Forest Ranch housewife's with a husband, children and a home to take care of but on some days we put on our riding gear and rode our motorcycles. I rode a Yamaha 125 Enduro, and Marge Polkinghorne, my friend and neighbor, rode a Honda 100 Trail Special. We were tall, slim, young women with dark hair but with Levis, a jacket, boots, gloves and helmets on us, we looked more like young men or boys. Unless we took off our helmets even our neighbors don't recognize us.

This time we were checking out a trail on the right side of Highway 32. We were several miles above the town of Forest Ranch, when we found this neat old logging road. We had never tried this one before. It was barely visible, almost buried by many years of pine needles, stick and leaves but it was new to us and off we went. I was in the lead as usual. My excitement mounted as the trail turned towards Butte Creek Canyon. If we could find a shortcut to the creek, oh what fun that would be!

It was a beautiful fall day with wonderful autumn colors surrounding us everywhere even overhead. The morning air felt fresh and cool as we rode along, going back and forth on the switchbacks. It was a standing on the pegs, sliding kind of riding, with sharp curves and slippery in the pine needles, take it easy on the front, wheel brakes or down you go! She was close behind me and what a thrilling ride it was. This new road was really going somewhere. Where it would possibly lead us I wasn't too sure but I LOVED the fun and excitement of it. However the one thing that I knew was, I could NEVER return back this way because it was way too steep and slippery and I wasn't that good of a rider and she wasn't as good as I.

I was sure by now; we were definitely heading towards Butte Creek Canyon. We had to make it down this way! Wheee, it was going to be a one way ride! Then we were at the bottom of the mountain and on the road alongside of Butte Creek. Everything was absolutely beautiful down here! It was all O.K. I knew the way home from here, just follow the creek downstream and get on Doe Mill Road, then onto Garland and back home we could go, but around the corner and whoops, we came to a tall gate which blocked our way. We found it was unlocked but on top was a sign which said, "NO TRESSPASSING!" What to do? We both agreed there was NO going back! We cautiously entered the gate and into what appeared to be somebody's large graveled back yard.

Steve and Jeff, our teenaged sons, had both warned us about a cranky retired sheriff who lived all by himself along that side of the creek. He had been really nasty and even threatened to arrest them for riding along there. We wanted to avoid him at all possible and find another way home.

"We cannot go back Marge, so lets' close this gate behind us and go on ahead." I said.

"What if they have big dogs in here?" said Marge. She was normally a rather shy and quiet person, but now she was starting to look a bit alarmed.

We could see the house through the trees, maybe no one is home and we can slip by. We were both slowly and quietly pushing our motorcycles now. Then there he stood in his sheriff's uniform with two big dogs. He was holding a rifle and packing a pistol on his hip. I was thankful he held the dogs back but he angrily shouted, "What are you guys doing in here?"

We took off our helmets, jackets and gloves, and gave him a big smile and a pleasant, "Good morning."

Then he changed completely. "Well, good morning," he said. "It is really quite O.K. if you ladies want to ride through here but first you must come in for some coffee and cookies." We both looked at each other, and I knew she was thinking the same thing as I that we did not want to go into his house and have coffee and cookies. Why would we trust this strange man? But we didn't want to be in trouble for trespassing either. We began politely talking to him about the weather and the pretty fall colors and so forth.

He said, "Park your motorcycles right here and I'll go make us some coffee."

"Well sir," I asked, "Is your wife home?"

"Oh yes, I think she is in there somewhere," he replied. As he walked towards the house, and stepped inside. Quickly glancing around we saw the front gate we needed to go through to get back on the main road and OUT of there.

"Come on Marge, put your helmet on and let's get through that gate!" I said. We hurriedly pushed our bikes towards that direction but the gate was securely padlocked. Frantically looking for another way out, I noticed a gape under the fence just beyond the left side of the gate. There was a shallow ditch down there.

"Marge, can you pull up that wire fence? I think I can get my bike under that fence!" I laid my bike down on top of my jacket and carefully slid it along the bottom of the ditch. It was all I could do and she had to get down in the ditch with me and help, but we got it under the fence. Then we ran back and got her bike, and did it again. We both quickly jumped on and started coasting down the hill. It was just in time. Then he came with the dogs wildly barking, and him waving and yelling at us. But we were down the road and gone! Would he jump in his truck and follow us? We stared our engines and ducked onto a side road shortcut to throw him off, just in case he did.

Back home after I drove my motorcycle into the garage and shut the garage door, I put on my apron and started dinner and so forth. We had decided not to tell anyone about our ride because we felt embarrassed about our trespassing (even if it was not intentional). Later that night my young daughter Brenda asked me if I liked being just a housewife. I winked at her and replied, "Yes sweetie, really do. Sometimes I have more fun than you know."

Later, Marge and I laughed a lot about our motorcycle escape but we never took THAT trail again. We never found the strange cave either. But we had a lot more really GREAT rides looking for it.

The Hummingbird

ADVENTURES IN CHICO
BY WILMA R. FORESTER

Summer in Chico, CA can be hot! Maybe even in the hundreds and on this July morning, it had already climbed into the eighties like another usual scorcher to be. I was living with some friends in their lovely two-story home. My friends were sincere Christian people and very nice to be around, but I really wanted to be in my own home. Because of recent bitter relationship problems that I won't go into detail about, I couldn't be home ever again. I told myself it would be all right, and I would be better off some day but I still woke in the wee hours of the night with tightness in my chest and panicky insecure feelings. The only good thing I could see happening to me these days was I prayed a lot more, and it made me feel closer to God.

The shop building I had just stepped into was much larger and nicer than most. It had a ceiling that went to a peek at about thirty-five feet or more with several Plexiglas skylights. It was a metal building, filled with motorcycles, fishing gear, car parts and a wooden bed project that Jerry, the owner, had been working on plus the normal collection of things that Sue, the wife, had added here and there. My saddle and riding gear were stored in the back corner of this large building. As I hurried to get my things to go horseback riding before it got too hot, something zipping about in the very top of the building caught my eye.

Oh no! It was a hummingbird trying desperately to get out thru the skylights. It flew from one skylight to the other, beating his head and wings against the glass again and again in a futile attempt to find a way to escape. Oh, poor panicking creature, how did you get in here? You won't last long up there in that heat in those spider webs. Then I thought how much like me it was, and I knew I had to try and save it, but how? Maybe a long stick with a net on the end, but where could I find one? And even if I did find one long enough, could I move it fast enough to scoop him into it? I knew hummingbirds were delicate and have to drink flower nectar often or they die quickly. How long had this bird been in here?

The small door I had entered was a dark solid one and it was hard to see that way out even if it was wide open. Anyway the wind had almost blown it shut by now. I started quietly talking to myself, "Oh well, control yourself Wilma. It is just a bird, and right now you have more important things to worry about than this unfortunate bird. It will soon curl up and die all alone, in the dust, on a rafter in the heat." Suddenly I blurted out LOUD, "Oh God, please be with this little tiny helpless bird somehow!" In frustration I stretched out my arms towards the sky as I said these words. The hummingbird stopped banging against the glass and looked towards me, and within a second he swooped down and landed on my right index finger. His tiny toes clamped on tight and he stared right into my face. Was this real? What was happening? Never in my life had I even heard of a wild bird landing on someone's hand! It just swished down and landed on me for no reason! If I move to the door, will he stay with me or just fly off to the ceiling again? As I stared at this beautiful, tiny, brilliantly colored, feathered creature, I felt weak in the knees unable to believe that he was still sitting on my finger, staring at me! Just then a slight breeze blew the shop door all the way open. On sneaking light feet, I finally dared to move very slowly towards the open door. I was quietly praying it would stay open and he would stay with me. He did!

We moved together out into the open, blue, cloudless sky and with not so much as a glance on my way, he was soaring upward to freedom. It felt like my heart went right along with him.

I stood there several minutes unable to believe what had just happened. You might think, oh well big deal, so a bird landed on your hand? Well, how many wild birds have landed on your hand? To me, it will always be a wonderful sign of encouragement just when I needed it, like a tiny, glowing angel soaring down to land on my outstretched hand, a sign from God my Father, a small miracle that I will never forget. God knows and cares about me, and sent a magic moment with a tiny hummingbird! It reminded me that God sent a lot more than that. He sent His only Son! "For God so loved the world (you and I are included in there) that he gave his only begotten Son that whosoever believeth in Him should not perish but have everlasting" John 3:16

***Miracles, large and small, are all around us
so we need to be expecting them!***

My beautiful horse Sultan and I had a GREAT ride that day!

Forest Ranch - The Fourth Stop

SOME FOREST RANCH HISTORY
BY WILMA R. FORESTER

Tiny beads of morning frost were melting among the many beautiful spring flowers. There were fragrant lupines, scrambled-eggs, buttercups and redbud, as well as strong smelling buck brush all in bloom. The only sound was buzzing bees and the chirping melody of the wild birds. The only motion was floating butterflies rising and falling. Then a small group of Madiu Indian children came into view. They were skipping, along a well-worn trail. A trail, which wound lazily up from the grassy plains of the valley and gracefully curved along the rocky ridge. Down below the cliffs on their left was a rushing stream filled with spring melting snow and rain. With their bare foot stepping lightly over the mud puddles and between the rocks, their brown scantily dressed bodies were ignoring the cold. Giggling, laughing and playfully bumping each other, they were in the lead of several family groups of native people which were trudging up the hill with their baskets of food and blankets, and other such belongings following the "Trail to the Great Mountain". Suddenly one of the older boys jerked to a stop. "Someone is coming," he whispered. In a matter of seconds, they all scattered like a covey of quail into nearby buckbrush, behind the rocks and crouched under a small pine tree thicket, they all quietly disappeared.

Then a dog barked and the thumping vibrations of trotting horses could be felt underfoot. Two fur trappers and a yellow dog came into view. The trappers knowingly called off the dog and passed on down the trail expecting to meet the rest of the family.

The "Trail to the Great Mountain" was well known with people and animals passing back and forth from the valley floor to the Big Meadows, which lies beneath the Great Mountain (Lassen). The Indians often took several weeks or even months to work their way along this trail. They usually camped in old familiar spots, taking side trips for hunting and gathering as desired. Going into the higher country in the spring of the year and returning in the fall was optional, and many other tribal groups chose to stay in the valley all year around. There is no record of time for this annual occurrence. It was just a way of life for thousands of years. It was soon to change!

A trickle of fur trappers and frontiersmen-explorers appeared on the scene and began to increase in about 1750. Even by 1840, very few Americans had ever been into what is now called, the Sacramento Valley. Like maybe only one or two and John Bidwell was one of them. (There were a few Spanish, French, Irish and German, fur trappers, as well as others.) Several years later in about 1850, after the discovery of gold, he (General John Bidwell, as he was called by this time) formed the Humboldt Wagon Road Company. In 1863, General Bidwell started building the road, which mostly followed this same "Trail to the Great Mountain" and beyond. General Bidwell enlisted the help of all who would work for him and this included the Mexicans, Indians, Chinese and even prisoners from Oroville. It was a commercial venture for him and it was a toll road. These large supply wagons, pulled by as many as eighteen or twenty horses, would be filled with his own produce of flour, fruit, nuts, hides, handmade iron tools and etc. Plus, there were many other goods which came up the Sacramento River on steamboats from the larger towns and seaports south of Bidwells' Rancherea.

These wagons were bound for the then booming Humboldt Silver mines in Nevada. The narrow, rocky dirt road was built in less than a year but this new Humboldt Wagon Road soon had cattle herders, passenger coaches, and timber haulers going both ways along with the supply wagons. Then of course the places to stop for food, water, lodging and perhaps a change of horses, sprang up every few miles along the way.

When the wagons left Chico, the first stop for water was Hog Springs, then Ten Mile House was the second stop, the third stop was Fourteen Mile House and the Fourth stop along the road was Forest Ranch. This short story is about the road, and especially about the town and people of Forest Ranch. (My point of view)

In the fall of 1963, a very nervous young mother came to a ladies meeting in Forest Ranch. She was holding her five months old child and she didn't know anyone at the meeting. Most of the women were older, and some quite large and loud. They had been meeting together for years and were laughing and talking, and there were no other little children, much less babies. It was me, Wilma Rolls and my infant daughter Brenda. She was fussing and there was no place to put her, and I needed to feed her. I was nursing her and that was considered a bit uncivilized at that time. I felt very shy but I needed to have no fears.

"Here, sit right here by the fire and I will get a blanket," said Betty Ferguson.

"I'll get you a cup of coffee," said Kate Petersen.

"This is the only baby in town and we are so glad to have you and your family," said Charlie Nelsen.

"Can I hold her after you feed her?" said Emma Johnson. Wow, what a welcome we received from everybody. This was not like any ladies meeting I had ever been too. It was very easy to feel at home with the people of Forest Ranch. Other ladies at that meeting were: Barbara Jones, Jessie Bashore, Lois Pierce, Shirlon Dodge, Carolyn Roper, Lucile Lorraine, Kate Peterson, Leona Taggart and I may have missed a few.

It is now 2012 and I can think back on many events, happenings and people of the town. Not that I am an old timer or remember it all, in fact I moved to Paradise for several years in the eighties and then returned in the nineties. But I would like to share with you what I do remember and some of the research and tales I have gathered from others.

To be honest in 1940, I remember Lomo more than Forest Ranch. After hiding in the back of the car because I didn't want to look over the edge of the terrible, scary, narrow road, we would come to some houses and a small store. About a third of a mile above where the town is now before the highway cut through, there was a cement (Diamond Match) horse trough with loose pigs wallowing in the spring, which flowed continually into a big mud puddle right in the middle of the road. Behind this was the post office connected to a small store which doubled as a bar. The pigs were free to wander here and there. I always thought they would all get run over. I think that was Forest Ranch. (I was seven?) Then there was the other place (Lomo) on up the road with a little store. It had food, gas and water too. Note: It is completely gone now.

"Look out Willie you are going to get wet," said my dad. We had stopped at Lomo to get some snacks before going on to Deer Creek for a fishing trip. It was about 1940. My dad never missed much. He was quick to explore any new country and he loved to go fishing, and he seldom overlooked a chance to get a soda or candy bar on the way. Lomo was a little store and stopping place for water, gas, food, beer and so forth. Thirty miles from Chico up Deer Creek Highway, sitting on a little rise on the right of the main road was Lomo. It was the last stop before Butte Meadows, which was on the right side. Then there was beautiful Chico Creek and Deer Creek, which are both on up the continuing Scenic Deer Creek Highway to the left.

We were a family of five, and were very excited to be fresh out of Los Angeles, having just moved to Chico. The Anderson family was: Wesley, (dad) or Andy as he was sometimes called, Hazel (mom), Clinton (brother), Barbara (sister), and Wilma (me) plus our dog Boogie.

The Lomo dogs were barking and the ice-cold spring water squirted out of the broken pipes near the one old-fashioned gas pump. Nearly everyone got wet if you wanted a drink from the spring as I did. When my dad and I wandered into the shabby old store and over to the bar, the smell of home cooked beans pulled you right in and we had to have some. Mrs. and Mr. Wes Gray were the storeowners and lived there also. That day I noticed a baby, a large one on the floor in a playpen and I later learned it was John Gray (the Lomo kid). I met John about thirty years later and he became a good friend of the family, and helped build our local Forest Ranch Baptist Church. He was six foot three and three-hundred pound plus some, a real fun loving and joking guy. He died in the 1986 or so.

Over the years, we took several trips up Deer Creek Highway, sometimes going into Chester or stopping at Butte Meadows. My family liked to campout whenever we got the opportunity to do so. I always enjoyed the drive going up Hwy. 32, except for the scary parts. But I loved the view at Fourteen-Mile-House, the beautiful green meadows and flowing springs with several horses and a large tan colored barn. At that time, I never thought I would live here in Forest Ranch, even though I considered it a very pretty place. Most of my childhood was spent in Chico. It took a tragic accident to make that happen and for our family to move out of Chico. In 1951, I married Roy Gene Rolls and we had two sons before I was 20 years old. Two wonderful fun boys, James Steven and Gene Jeffery, and then Jim died in a hanging accident at age nine, and Jeff, who was seven, was often sick with asthma. Then in 1963, I had my girl Brenda Jean. She was a surprise because the Rolls family had a reputation for nearly all boys but I happily broke the spell. The doctors said Jeff would probably be better at a higher altitude and away from all the valley grasses. So Gene went looking for a higher, happier home for us.

More Rolls' family stories:

Gene Rolls and Bob Batt met with the local Forest Ranch realtor Claude Lorraine (Jim Palm's grandfather) in the summer of 1963. It was a hot summer and Mr. Lorraine showed them everything he had for sale and he was a shaker mover guy, and I think they bought some acreage out of exhaustion.

Bob said, "That old man wore me out!" We (both families) purchased several areas and divided it between us. It was between the New Highway 32 and an old branch of the original Humboldt Wagon Road. We later named the road, Sugar Pine Place. It was a beautiful spot with a view of the Chico lights at night, on our piece.

"A thousand dollars an acre!" The whole town was in shock. Then the Rolls family of four moved into the Forest Ranch apartments across from the old Forest Ranch School. It was owned by Dr. Erickson (Carl Finley's place now). We lived there for a year while our home was being built two miles up the road. Jack and Evelyn Culverhouse were the managers of the apartments. There were quite a few old apple trees behind the school (a few old ragged ones are still there) and when Dr. Erickson came up, we had no water because the spring on lower Schott Rd. supplied the apartments and the doctor would water his apple orchard all day. We never knew when that was going to happen. There was an old abandoned place up the little stream that was called The Lodge. It sat right over streambed (Lower Schott Rd. just a short walk above the old school). There was no power or potty facilities in this abandoned home but we got an old piano fixed and cleaned the place. We received permission to have a Good News Club there and most of the children from the school would walk with us to The Lodge after school every Friday and we would sing and tell Bible stories. I think loud singing and laughter woke up all the local squirrels, woodpeckers and even vibrated the trees. It was fun!

On the very first night at the apartments, Mr. Culverhouse gave Jeff (then ten years old) a small (wooden box) animal trap. Jeff put peanuts in it and set it in the pretty bird feeder to see what he might catch. The next morning, we trapped a flying squirrel. It was quite and beautiful with large brown eyes and very soft fur, and seemed completely unafraid of us. "Oh Mom, can I keep him, can I keep him, can I keep him?" He coaxed.

"Well Jeff, we caught him on the first try and I am sure you can catch all you want if you let him go," I said. He never caught another one after months and months of trying. Note: Flying squirrels are abundant in Forest Ranch but they only come out at night so you seldom get to see them. Several years later, we raised two tiny ones as pets. (Someone rescued them from the hole of a log on the way to the mill. They were delightfully playful and dove from us to the curtains back and so forth. When they were old enough, we made a box home for them, nailed it high in a tree on Schott Rd., and turned them loose.

After we built our home and move in, we were known as the richest family in Forest Ranch because we had a new car (company) and new house, and Jeff had a nice bicycle. That first November, we got three and half of snow and of course the power went off. I was concerned about elderly widow lady up the street, Mrs. German. I put on my boots and bundled up baby Brenda and myself, and went trudging through the snow perhaps to rescue her. Much to my surprise, she had a pot of beans on her little stove, a load of wood for the fire, her kerosene lamp going and her feet up reading a book. She taught me a lot. She showed me how to put milk and meat, and such outside in the snow (up high so the dogs couldn't get it) and have several bottles, buckets and such of clean water and a good load of wood before the storm came. Then just wait it out. The power could be off for a week or more in those days.

The school was the main event for everyone. If you have children there, of course you went to every event you could, but WOWEE, parents, grandparents, and most of the neighbors ALL went to EVERY event. The Forest Ranch children were the heart of the town. And anything needed was taken care of by the local people such as repairs or playground equipment help for the teacher. Some of the school events, if you didn't get there soon enough, you stood outside and looked in the windows because the place so crowded. There was a great feeling of pride and love for the children such as I had never seen in the schools of Chico. It was wonderful for the kids. My children, Jeff and Brenda loved it.

Grover Jones ran the service station which was located where the store is now. We had GAS in town! Grover pulled you out or fixed your car, often with no charge and was a very caring and helpful man. The School children even wrote a song about him and sang it to him in a school play. If you were a Forest Rancher, you were just IN and everyone was your friend.

Claude Willus (Well driller) was often sitting at the store waiting for someone to talk to. Then, there was Dan Hartley (more Well driller), Bill Fitzgerald (builder, developer) Nancy Grey (Pierce) great cook, Jack Lindbergh (more storyteller) and many more.

Highway 32 behind my house could be seen clearly from my kitchen window (the trees were smaller along there at that time). I was home with little Brenda a lot because Gene didn't want me to drive to Chico on that scary road and my car was pretty old. The cars on Highway 32 passed by so seldom that I would drop whatever I was doing, and run down the hill and see who was going to town and wave at them. I made little Brenda an Indian outfit, and she had a bow, arrows, moccasins, and all. With feathers in her hair she would run through the woods, and jump upon a stump and throw her arms open wide and sing "Born Free" and I thought it was very appropriate.

Jeff saved his money and bought an old Motor scooter for $25 dollars (which he had to completely rebuild). He was allowed to ride anywhere for miles around Forest Ranch, just stay off of the highway and don't run out of gas.

My parents, Wesley and Hazel Anderson, moved in on Wagon Road several years later (Mom chose the name of the road). Then along came my sister and brother-in-law, Barbara and Bob Batt, with their two sons Dan and Bill, they built their home and moved in on lower Sugar Pine Way. Soon after came my brother and sister-in-law, Clint and Donna Anderson and son Jim and daughter Sheri. Clint developed the Pine Way area and built his home there.

The Indians and John Bidwell have long ago disappeared, and the historic stops along the road are hard to spot. Many things have changed, people have come and gone but I am happy to say the little town of Forest Ranch, which was the Fourth Stop, is still here.

My name is Wilma Forester (Gubbels) now and I live on Wagon Rd. I have many good memories of the people then as well as now because, I love Forest Ranch, the FOURTH STOP.

Side Story: Beautiful Bess

My Daddy's Aunt Bess had some real heartaches and problems. It was several years after the great depression when Bess Heeb and her husband lost everything they had, money, business, friends etc. His very successful business in Chicago had completely failed. He could not deal with all the problems and jumped out the window of the top floor, fourteen stories up. It was rumored that young Bess had been so beautiful people would stop her on the street and asked to take her picture. However Bess was very helpless, spoiled and also a heavy smoker. Her son Calvin was about the same age as my brother Clinton (ten). She was broke and homeless with no place to go. Her sisters, friends, and relatives all looked the other way because Bess was a real potential problem for most anyone. What happened next still surprises me. When my Mother, (Hazel Anderson) heard about poor broken hearted Bess and her young son and she said, "Come to Chico and live with us, you and your son are most WELCOME here!" Note; they had never met!

You need to know there were five of us, plus two dogs, a cow and a horse. We lived in a small two bedroom house. Daddy was driving a delivery truck for a local Coca-Cola Co., and times were hard! When they came, my sister and I had to give up our bedroom and sleep in sleeping bags on the front room floor, so Aunt Bess could have some privacy.

Side story to my side story

One hot summer night, Bess was undressing for bed when she saw a man's face staring in the bedroom window. She screamed and my Daddy sprang into action. He chased the intruder (Peeking Tom) through our corn field and followed his footprints (it was muddy) right up to the front door of our neighbor Mr. K. Daddy (Wesley) banged on the locked door but no one answered. I knew that neighbor man was very fortunate that my Daddy didn't catch him. As far as we knew he never did that again and we never told on him.

Back to Aunt Bess: She couldn't do even simple things, like wash her clothes, do dishes, and clean her room, nothing. She also could not drive a car. Mom lovingly showed her how to be useful. Mom also took time to comfort and just be a friend to both of them. After just a few weeks Aunt Bess got a job at the Hotel Oaks on Main St. in Chico, she was making beds and cleaning rooms. It was hard work and low pay but it was the only thing she knew how to do. She not only did her job well but she saved her money and got an apartment, on her own, for herself and her son Calvin. We found out later, Calvin had a brilliant mind, and even though he rode a bike to school, he never missed a day and made straight A's. Aunt Bess never remarried; she lived the rest of her life with her son, who later became a Nuclear Physicist.

My mom was quick to show true Christian love even if it cost her. Aunt Bess and Calvin were forever grateful to her. We kids learned what it means to be a REAL friend. Note: My cousin Calvin was also a lot of fun to play with.

Side Story: The Swimming Pool

My sister Barbara had BIG dreams. She wanted a swimming pool a real Hollywood type cement pond. Nobody had a pool in those days (only movie stars). We lived in the sticks on Cactus Ave. The soil where our house sat was like cement, it was called Hard Pan. Poor Daddy was often out of work and we finally managed to get an indoor toilet put in the house, but Barbara WANTED a swimming pool! So one hot summer day, when she asked him again, Daddy said "O.K. Sister, as he called her, show me where you want it and let's talk about it."

We went outside and she pointed to one side of the house where she wanted her pool to go. Dad said, "Well let's just measure it out and figure out what we have to do." They measured and then marked off the space with rocks. "First we have to have the hole," he said. He went and got a shovel, pick, and a bucket for the dirt and showed her how to dig. He told her when she got the hole done they would plan out the rest of it. Now Barbara doesn't like to get dirty and she hates dirt but she and I spent many days working on the pool. She wouldn't come and play with me if I didn't help her work on the pool. Well, we never got a swimming pool but she never asked Daddy about it again either.

Side Story: Clint and the Bodybuilder

We seldom had books or magazines in our house when we lived on Cactus Ave. in Chico but on occasion we got the Farm Journal. My brother Clinton, who was three years older than I, was tall and thin. I think he was also getting pushed around a bit at school. One morning, he saw a picture of Charles Atlas on the back of the Farm Journal. Charles Atlas was a musclebound bodybuilder, often posing like he was holding up the whole World on his back. Well Clint wanted a Weight- Lifting set so he could look like Charles Atlas.

"Please Dad, I really need to have this or I just know I will be thin and weak ALL of my life." Almost every morning he would ask Dad again about it. So one day my Dad said, "Clint I have been thinking about this and I have an idea. One time I heard about a man who became a great bodybuilder and this is what he did, he got a young calf and every morning he would lift the calf upon his shoulders and put it down again and as the calf grew the man grew stronger and stronger too and by the time the calf was a big bull the man could still go out and lift him." Dad continued. "Betty Lou (our cow) will be having her calf very soon so you can do the same thing"

Well, Clint's eyes lit up at this story and when Betty Lou had her calf, Clint was ready. Before school every morning, he put on his boots (sometimes it was a real mess out there) and caught the little calf and lifted it a few times. This went on for several week or more, but soon the calf didn't want to be lifted and Clint had to chase it through the mud trying to catch it. Then the calf grew so very fast and soon he couldn't lift it any more.

So much for that idea! But he never asked for a weight lifting set again. Note: In spite of all his worrying, Clint grew up to be a very handsome, well-built man of six feet two and weighed more than two hundred lbs. Perhaps it was milking Betty Lou, but I think it was mostly shoveling all that manure that did it.

Side Story: Rainbow Island

"Let's take our dolls and go to RAINBOW ISLAND," I said to my sister Barbara, we were perhaps, ten (Wilma) and eleven (Barbara). It was our favorite thing to do! Now Rainbow Island only existed after a good rain and usually it had an abundance of wild flowers everywhere. It was just a small lava rock formation, located in a gully with a little stream running through it. But in the spring after it rained, it became our magic Rainbow Island. It was located in the open, rocky plains leading up to the foothills, West of our home on Cactus Ave, in Chico, There was no one else around, just two girls with rag dolls and their imaginations. Sometimes Brownie (dumb Brownie), our dog followed along.

How it started: We had no dolls! Barbie Dolls had not been invented, there was no plastic until about1947or so. Oh, Mom bought us some tall, stiff, pressed wood dolls for Christmas years ago but they were getting a little tired and chipped, and the legs and arms were ridged. One boring summer day, we got this bright idea! We collected some of daddy's socks, along with cotton stuffing, a needle and lots of thread, and make what to us were amazingly fun dolls. It took several afternoons but when we finished they were about the size of the nowadays Barbie Dolls. WOW, they could bend, sit, swim, twist, ride horses and move in any direction, and they were soft to touch. We even put boobs on them, an unheard thing in that day. "Betty," her doll, was a blue eyed blonde and "Nancy," my doll, was a green eyed brunette. Both had thick, long, thread hair that we could pin up, let it dry and comb into beautiful long curls.

When playing with them at home, we would set out the washtub, fill it with water and that became their swimming pool. We sat around the tub and using our imaginations, wooden blocks, rocks, chicken feathers, oak balls and of course Mom's sewing scraps, they all became houses, furniture, cars, clothes, horses, kids, dogs, and etc. We also made two boyfriends for them, but they were much plainer. (Tom and what's his name?)

The real fun began when we were out picking wildflowers one day and stumbled upon Rainbow Island. If you sat down below the small waterfall and looked up through the spray, it made a Rainbow, thus the name. In the middle of the two-foot deep pool was a nice rock Island. Nancy and Betty were at their most thrilling best at Rainbow Island. They had Indian attacks, birthday parties, western adventures, weddings, canoe rides with dangerous alligators, many romantic encounters, and everything but John Wayne and sometimes HE came too. Also, if it was a very hot day, we weren't past stripping off and taking turns in the pool ourselves. (Move over Brownie!)

Sad ending: Betty, Nancy, and their boyfriends all drown in the bottom of our family well. Our Brother Clint was mad at us, for some reason. (I think he felt left out at times.) He told us later, "They screamed all the way down." We never made any new ones, but to us they were MUCH nicer than the current Barbie Dolls that little girl of today play with. Anyway, after a good rain and up at Rainbow Island, our homemade rag dolls really came to life and it was the best FUN ever!

Side Story: Tilly Come Home

"Quick someone call the Hwy. Patrol because there is a black horse running down the road heading to Oroville." (Of course no one had cell phones yet)

My friend La Donnas' beautiful black mare had a strange habit. At least several times a year when she felt like being a mother again, she would run away. When Donna and I rode together, my horse Buck would jump over logs and so forth but Tilly would never JUMP anything. Then when she got it into her head to find the Stallion she would circle the field faster and faster and over a high fence she would go. La Donna lived near us in the Pleasant Valley area of Chico, on Mariposa Ave. All on her own, her horse Tilly would jump the fence, go across town and take Hwy. 99 to Oroville at a gallop.

People would stop their cars and try to catch her but no one ever did. She would out maneuver them and end up at the horse farm in Oroville, where her boyfriend lived. The folks who lived there would call up La Donnas' parents, Mr. or Mrs. Turner and tell them Tilly is here again. She was a small pretty gaited mare and Mr. Turner who went to bring her home was very large, almost three-hundred pounds. Since they had no horse trailer, he took the saddle and bridle, and had someone drive him over there so he could ride her back home. The return trip was along the highway at a fast clip the same way she had come. People seeing them often called out to him," Why don't YOU carry the horse?"

It always amazed me that Tilly knew the way through Chico. Note: there was no overpass through Bidwell Park at that time. She had to avoid all the traffic and find the right roads. It never seemed to hurt her to go over and back in one day. I don't know if she was running away from home or back to it. I have heard of dogs and some cats finding the way over long distances but horses usually just find their way to a spot of grass and that is all they care about. It made me think of the story of "Lassie Come Home". Lassie wasn't the only smart one. "Tilly comes home," I thought she was almost as smart as Lassie.

Side Story: Chickens and Sweet peas

We were the people in the old farm house with the barn and windmill on Cactus Ave. in Chico, CA. We raised chickens and rabbits, and sold eggs and milk (from our cow Betty Lou) to many of our neighbors

Mom had an incubator that would hatch out hundreds of chicks at a time. When they were old enough, the whole family would work at the dirty job of butchering them. Daddy would kill them and hand one to me and one to Barbara. We sat on a low stool near a bucket of hot water, dipped the chicken in the water for about one minute and tore off all the feathers. You must start at the tail first because the big tail feathers are the hardest to get out. Pick them clean and don't tear the skin. Take them to Mom and get another one. And start over. Mom learned to clean them out in one smooth move. She wrapped them in waxed paper (plastic showed up about 1947) and then newspaper and Clint, the lucky guy got to deliver them. We had rabbits also but because they squealed, Dad could not bring himself to kill them. So we turned them all loose.

Side story to side story

The rabbits quickly went wild. They dug holes near the barn and had their babies underground. Every spring I would set very still beside the holes and sometimes, I could catch the adorable baby Bunnies. I loved to play with them and then turn them loose again. There were wild rabbits mixed with our colorful spotted rabbits all over the country side for many years.

Mom loved to work in the yard and garden. I have yet to taste better tomatoes than what she grew. The soil was not the best. (It was called hard pan) but with enough digging, and with cow and chicken manures, she made it work.

One rainy year, she started digging way before springtime and planted something all along the fence and around the whole front yard. Then she covered the seeds with newspapers, cardboard and put boards on top of that. I thought she was crazy because it was so muddy and cold. What could possibly come from all this work? Before Mother's Day that spring, we had thousands of sweet peas. Just before the big day, she put an ad in the Chico Paper. People came by the dozens for bouquets of sweet Peas. They had grown over six feet tall on both sides of the fence. She cut and sold so many flowers she got tired and quit. But Barbara and I kept on cutting the last of the sweet peas and handing them out to people. We made so much money I couldn't believe it, (about twenty dollars each). Of course Mom made much more! I was amazed how well it paid off and that the people from town could find our little place. We were considered to be way out in the country at this time. The flowers were so beautiful, plus they scented up the whole outdoors. I still love sweet peas.

Side Story: The Trophy or What is Falling?

In my early twenties, I had a very nice horse which I seldom rode. I had two young sons whom I was having too much fun with. So, I loaned my horse to a neighbor Vern Grider who was an excellent horseman. Vern had just gotten a job herding cattle and being a real working cowboy at Richardson Springs, which is a beautiful resort area near Chico. However, he didn't have a horse to ride and I knew my horse would come back better trained and in great shape, if Vern was using him. I loved horses and riding, and always wanted to be a horse trainer but that would have to wait. In the spring when my horse-Buddy-came back, he was so well behaved and fun to ride, I decided to enter him in the Chico Riding Club Horseshow. This was a state recognized show and if you were a serious competitor there was work to do on me and the horse. I knew I would be competing against several horse training centers and real professional riders.

SIDE STORY: THE TROPHY OR WHAT IS FALLING?

Also, I would need some special equipment which I didn't have, like chaps, spurs, rope, hat, gloves, silver bit, plus a fancy bridle and saddle. I begged and borrowed everything I could, and just made do with the rest. I worked with my horse and my riding seat every evening. When the day of the show came, I washed, clipped and shined my quarter horse to perfection. He was a light chestnut color with a flaxen mane and trail, a white star and snip on his face, and he looked just beautiful. I dressed myself in all that gear; I had no fancy saddle and rode to the show (no horse trailer). Most of the contestants had assistants and helpers plus extra equipment and so forth but in my case it was just me and my horse. I loved the Western Pleasure Class and that is what I entered.

When my event started, there were about 15 or 16 other riders competing. They played the music and the announcer told us what to do. Buddy, perfectly calm and obedient, was giving me sliding stops and swinging turns, and soon we were down to just three competing riders. I was thrilled to be still in there! I knew I would at least get a third place ribbon. Even after a hand gallop (very fast run) Buddy was working on a loose rein, perfectly. Then there were only two of us. I was talking to myself trying to remember what to do and keep calm. The announcer called the two of us to stand in front of the judge, while he slowly examined our horses with a white gloved hand. They must be perfectly groomed. Mr. Hains, the other contestant was riding a large bay stallion with a magnificent silver saddle and I knew HE was a real working horseman.

The judge scratched his head in indecision and asked us to take the ring to the left, repeating the canter again. We both started out in the proper lead, going perfectly and then SOMETHING HAPPENED! The middle strap on my chaps came loose and they were slipping down my legs about to fall off on both sides. OOHH HELP, what to do? I carefully lay my reins down on Buddy's neck while I let the rhythm of my body tell him to keep cantering. Then I reached down and pulled up my chaps and retied them again. Buddy NEVER missed a step. The watching crowd cheered and applauded. Mr. Haines's bay stallion flinched at the sound and switched into the wrong lead. The judge called me in and handed me the First Place TROPHY! Yes, Buddy was a terrific horse and I have to say thanks to Vern Grider. But guess what, now I have two trophies, because the next year Buddy and I DID it again! P. S. I kept my chaps ON this time!

Meet Me at the Gate

Would you please meet me at the gate? I mean the old weathered, wooden gate by the edge of the meadow. We can run down the hillside and chase or catch whatever we find in the tall grass and among the wild flowers, just like we did before. There may be little rabbits and beautiful butterflies. It will be so fun. Let's take a snack and sit on top of the mountain a while. I am so glad you are not always cleaning your house or going to town shopping like all the others. We are different you and I, we don't just talk about how to clean the bathroom or what to shop for or cook for dinner tonight. We have real outdoor adventures and exciting things to do. Yes, please meet me at the old wooden gate in the meadow, however, I may be a little late so don't wait for me too long because I have to stop at Wal-Mart's first. They are having a sale!

By Wilma R. Forester

Just a Boy

Jesus, were you ever just a boy? Did you have wavy brown hair when you were a child? So many artists have painted you that way. What color were your eyes? Did you play in the sand, and run up and down the little hills just like children in the ages of time before and after you have done? Was there a ball to throw and chase after? Did you enjoy a pet? Maybe you had a puppy or young burro to play with? Did your hair shine in the sun as you laughed with other children? If you had a fall did you cry real tears?

What about favorite food? Did your mother Mary make a cake on your birthday or perhaps it was a special loaf of bread? Did you feel loved and sheltered by your earthly parents, and were you ever lonely? How soon did you know who you were and why you had come?

Many things we do not know about you but this we do know, Jesus you became the Christ who died for all of us! So that we could know the awesome love of the Heavenly Father who sent you to earth and for a little while let you be just a boy.

Wilma R. Forester

The Truth

We as human beings do not choose where, what time in the history of the world, what race, what gender, what intelligence, what parents or siblings or the order of birth, what state of poverty or wealth we are born into, or what health we will have.

We have little control over how long we live. We are born helpless and completely dependent on someone to care for us. The care must be years of nurture and protection if we survive. Even with this care some live minutes, some days, some years, and a few live to a hundred and a bit more but all die. Many infants are killed before or shortly after birth. All of us are controlled by time and gravity, and human weakness. We are not strong physical creatures compared to the animal world around us. Our strongest point is our reasoning abilities but this is also a weakness and contributes to greed and fear.

We do not know where we come from at conception or where we go at death. We often have strong bonds with each other. We call it love, but often it is need and dependence on one another. There is a very strong desire to survive and procreate,

Many of us are quite different from one another in sensitivity, reasoning, size and shape, color of skin and body type. All of us have the same basic needs for food, shelter, water, and sanitation. We are a gregarious group by nature and have a strong need for acceptance and approval of each other.

We are often bound together in groups, large or small by culture or race. One group will hate and kill another, and be held in high esteem for doing it. When the races and cultures are forced to mix, they lose their identity and there is fighting and bad feelings. Education and knowledge about each other helps to overcome this but does not eliminate it.

Desire for wealth and power are very strong in most individuals. Pride and greed are common and even boundless in some people. Individuals or groups who have little possessions or food often become servants to the ones who have more. Those in control (with power and possessions) make up the rules for all to live by (governments). This is done to insure their governmental control and also to protect the poor and weak from stronger groups and from each other. However the controlled groups always find ways around these laws and break them more and more if they are to survive and assert themselves. Then new and more laws have to be set up but no politics, legislatures, or philosophies can force a man to change his basic nature and so man's inhumanity to man continues.

Because governments make it possible for the poor groups to survive and procreate, and because of many scientific advances against disease, many weak and sickly survive that in natural settings would not. This contributes to millions and millions of people often in one area making it even more difficult to control the diseases and provide sanitation and have enough food for all. These people are often at the mercy of wars, plagues, drought and floods, etc. When or if these poor groups become strong, they often kill and overthrow the controlling group, taking what they have and then they become the controlling group and so it continues.

We people of this world use the plants and animals for food and skins, etc. By caging and killing millions of animals, whole species of creatures and plant life have been wiped from the earth. Often the animal killing is for sport or entertainment only.

We tend to destroy and pollute the world we live in by overuse of the natural resources and changing the surroundings to fit our need or greed without considering the results it causes to nature. We live as though we are the only one in the universe that counts.

Many cultures and religions are set up which try to combat this destructive path but history shows that humans do not change. The only notable or seemingly permanent change in the basic nature of man the world has ever seen is in the form of Christianity. Religion has caused more death suffering and wars than anything else on earth but true Christianity is not a manmade religion but God reaching down to all mankind, the haves and the have-nots as well. The author of true love is God and in his love God sent His only Son to die for all of the above problems plus the basic sinful selfish nature of man. He wrote it down in a love letter to all of us! (The Holy Bible) Believing in God and receiving what He has done thru the Lord Jesus Christ is the only hope for humans to have a change of heart.

This can make you happy or sad, you can try to change it or not, but it is the truth and you are a part of it, if you are human.

Life's Inviting Trails

There are many trails stretching out before me, but leading where?

How many hooves, paws, or footprints have pressed into the earth here?

And what kind of creature first decided which way this path would lead?

Maybe my journey could be shortened by going a bit to the left or easier going turned more toward the right, yes I think there is a light up over that hill side there.

But right now there are rough branches in my face and rocks sprinkled along the ground ahead of me.

Excited to start, I anxiously stretch up tall, trying to see where this trail will take me, and inside my heart I asked myself, am I ready, SHOULD I go?

Then it occurs to me that I may need a MAP, and I've heard GOD has one!

About the Author-Artist
Wilma R. Anderson, Rolls, Forester (Gubbels)

"Wilma you are going to get an A on the story you wrote in your High School English class," said my teacher. Wow I didn't make very many A's, so I was surprised. "Maybe someday you will become a writer," she continued. I didn't think so. I was just too much into riding and training my horse and chasing boys.

I was born in L.A. CA in 1933 and we had NO books at home to read. Most books were very expensive and our family just couldn't afford things like that. But one day my father bought a new set of encyclopedias called The Book of Knowledge. There were at least ten books and even at five years old I loved every one of them. Even though I couldn't read, I would spend hours going through the pages and studying the pictures and enjoying the Aesop Fables. I scribbled my first horse inside the cover of one of the new books (shame on me) and instead of a whipping my Dad said, "Wow Willy, I can't draw a horse like that and you can't even write your name yet." He got me some drawing paper and art pencils.

ABOUT THE AUTHOR-ARTIST

We, the Anderson family, Mom, Dad and three kids plus our dog Boogie, moved to Chico in 1940. We lived in several different places and finally settled in the barren wastelands of the eastern part of town called Pleasant Valley. Ours was one of only two houses on Cactus Ave. My older brother Clinton, my sister Barbara, and I usually walked the two miles to the one room Pleasant Valley School. It was great horse country and easy to access Bidwell Park. I am still writing stories about my many childhood adventures in Chico and Bidwell Park.

I married very young and had two sons and later a daughter. James Steven(deceased), Gene Jeffrey and Brenda Jean. The R.G. Rolls family moved to Forest Ranch in 1964. I married Jacques Gubbels in 1997 and we still live in Forest Ranch, CA. I go by the name of Wilma Rae Forester, which is also my artist name. I have trophies and ribbons from riding and painting but being a Christian: To you O Lord, I lift up my soul: in you I trust, O my God. Psalm 25:1-2, and my children, grandchildren and great grandchildren are the things I boast about the most.

I am an artist first of all but I also love to write, whether it is fiction or non-fiction. Of course, I get to illustrate all of my stories. Sometimes when I am deep into telling a tale, it feels like I have stepped into another world and it is a wonderful world of privacy and freedom where I alone am in control. I truly enjoy writing and painting.

Wilma R. Forester

www.ingramcontent.com/pod-product-compliance
Lightning Source LLC
LaVergne TN
LVHW070533070526
838199LV00075B/6770